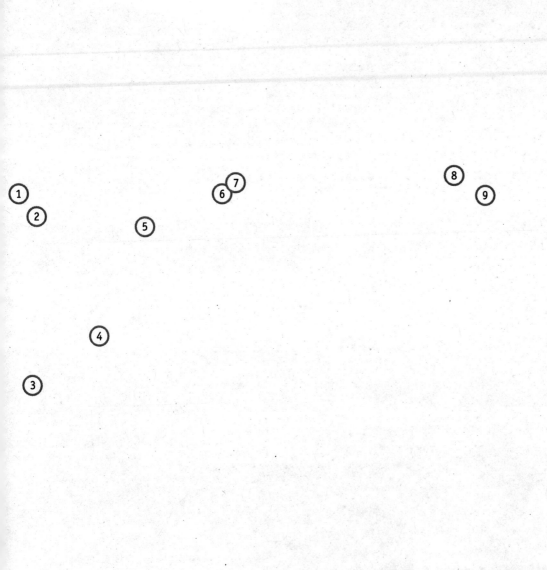

14 Tractors

NeWest Press

Tractors

14

The Man From Saskatchewan, Book 3
poems by Gerald Hill

Best wishes to all who read here.

Copyright © Gerald Hill 2009

Library and Archives Canada Cataloguing in Publication

Hill, Gerald, 1951-
    14 tractors / Gerald Hill.
Poems.
Includes bibliographical references.
ISBN 978-1-897126-39-4
I. Title. II. Title: Fourteen tractors.
PS8565.I443F68 2009   C811'.54   C2008-907031-3

Editor for the Board: Douglas Barbour
Cover and interior design: Natalie Olsen
Cover illustration: Natalie Olsen
Author photo: Amy Snider

NeWest Press

201.8540.109 Street
Edmonton, Alberta T6G 1E6
780.432.9427
newestpress.com

No bison were harmed in the making of this book.
NeWest Press is committed to protecting the environment and to the responsible use of natural resources. This book was printed on 100% post-consumer recycled paper.

1 2 3 4 5 12 11 10 09

printed and bound in Canada

NeWest Press acknowledges the support of the Canada Council for the Arts, the Alberta Foundation for the Arts, and the Edmonton Arts Council for our publishing program. We also acknowledge the financial support of the Government of Canada through the Book Publishing Industry Development Program (BPIDP).

In memory of Brother Bernard Lange, O.S.B.,
1929 – 2004

Let the Abbot appoint brethren on whose life and character he can rely, over the property of the monastery in tools, clothings, and things generally, and let him assign to them … all the articles which must be collected after use and stored away…. [No one shall] handleth the goods of the monastery slovenly or carelessly.

The Rule of St. Benedict
Chapter XXXII
"Of the Tools and Goods of the Monastery"

When should the drawbar be fastened, when allowed to swing?

Fundamentals of Machine Operation
John Deere Tractors

we will not drown in this july air
tho one hurls one's lines
as a drowning man
or a falling fool
might

bpNichol
The Martyrology, Book 5

Contents

A Few Words at First Light
Knowing
What You Think About on the Tractor
Getting to Tractors
Tractor Exhibition (Entrance)
                              (Exit)
Tractor Day
Getting Satisfaction
Chapter Quiz I

Tractor Kid Number Seven
How I Cleaned the Tractor Cab
Family Day at the Case-New Holland Dealership
(Dream of) My Bride's Demeanour
Eighteen Miles Southeast of Avonlea
Hope, Part One
Notes for a Verse Heard on CHAB
Favourite Time of Day
Chapter Quiz II

Part I
July

LEFT

FRONT

REAR

RIGHT

The Poet:

*You must have, what, five or six
tractors out here?*

Brother Bernard, farm manager:

We've got 14 tractors.

Why so many tractors?
Well why give them away.
They run. They don't cost us anything.

I bought the Steiger CM-350 in Humboldt a year old.
Rubber's getting a little wore out.

A toy compared to what some farmers have.

250 hp
6000 hours
34,000 pounds
600 ft-lbs. lugnut torque
strawberry air freshener in the cab

We should have one twice as big.

Air-conditioned? Oh
it would have to be.

To see the Steiger in the field which ends, hori-
zon blazing with dust, is to see
marks a morning pulls from a day.

The Steiger sails off southeast,
appears to be not coming back.
It survives horizons, after being one
and repeating itself for hours.

The Steiger loops, heads north again.

John Deere 8100, a beautiful machine.
Pulls a combine, airdrill, cultivator, stonepicker.
Used for seeding.
Stable on hillsides with those duals.

A hundred and sixty horses,
I can drive it all day.

It's a beautiful machine.

In the heat surrounded by tractors
I am not afraid for there be torque
amps and maintenance logs
and thousands of deep red hours
and diesel-friendly heavens made of cloud.

And when love breaks down reach in
a toolbox, give yourself a hammer,
new belt, a rag, a couple of hours off.

The clouds, noon breeze, bad old blue —
all in their own little world
while I'm
thanks to tractors
in mine.

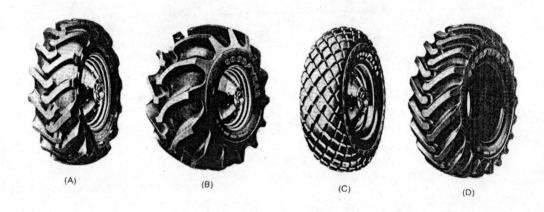

(A) (B) (C) (D)

When I got here in 1947 we had only two tractors, an old Case
and a W30 International
and 18 horses.

This is the 784.
Front-end loader work: snow, barrels, gravel.
A simple, straightforward diesel from Humboldt.

With a loader tractor you can't see what's happening in front.
It was damaged during the moving of a big tree.
It was abused, in plain English.

They run, they're paid for, they do
a million jobs
leaving few for the rest of us.

They're deeply indifferent machines
but if a beautiful woman cycles by
in a new shirt she bought in town
and consignment khakis the tractors
turn gentlemen alert for what
they can do for her this morning,
accustomed, as they are, to grooming
the earth in style.

Get a tractor started, it will not stop
talking for hours, automatic, that's how
it works, don't let her ever
see you still.

The 4430 has been stonepicking, baling, and grinding feed,
standing there since seeding time.

On its second set of rubber but the motor hasn't been touched.

Trouble Shooting

Engine emits black smoke:
clogged or dirty aircleaner,
see your John Deere dealer.

Engine emits white smoke:
defective thermostat,
see your John Deere dealer.

Engine emits grey smoke:
winter in it, air the colour of echo.

Engine emits red smoke:
blood in it.

Engine emits yellow smoke:
out-takes from hell's half-ochre, exhausted.

Engine emits blue smoke:
longing for the summer life
of intake, sky all air.

Tractors mostly in air you'd think
they derive from clouds
and some of them drive like clouds
the blue drifts grey, wind-like,
before and after rain.

About chirp-high the breeze
lifts again a rush
and ruckus of leaves east
and beyond that east.

The International Harvester 300 Utility, the 300,
was the main tractor 20,000 hours ago
around the time of the provincial jubilee.

It's sweet as a jubilee apple
in the queen's right hand.

> *Bale*
> *combine*
> *spray*
> *harrow*
> *bind,*

> *main job now —*
> *dig potatoes.*

I was offered a good price for it.
It's not only antique but rare,
so I touch up the paint from time to time.

The Basics in the Tool Kit

set of flat wrenches
hammer (a definite must)
screwdriver
crescent wrench

And rags. When you work with hydraulics
you've always got something on your hands.

But as long as you have a pocket knife
you can get any tractor started.
I use mine every day.

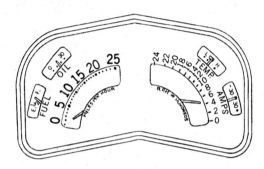

Fig. 3 — Tachometer And Speedometer Can Be Separate Instruments

When everything grows what do you do?
Get a bigger tractor probably used
from a dealer in a nearby town.
So the 300 Utility, once
the biggest tractor anywhere,
the size of two Harleys in a deep red shell,
becomes so small it's rare.

Put your shortwave on the torso
of the 300 you get Johannesburg,
Tulsa, Cape Cod with all reception
clear but the minute you move the radio
from the tractor's invisible radiance
some salesman in Los Angeles
breaks in and out, traffic that
draws you away.

Reach your hand toward a tractor, tune in.

*The 724 built in Germany
hauls a 1000-gallon water tank
from the dugout to the garden
or the honey wagon.*

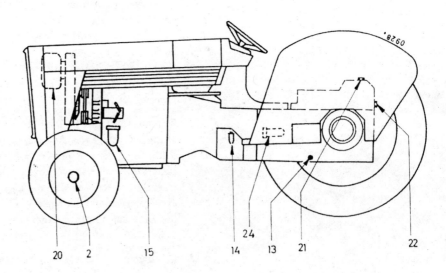

The W-4 Standard, bought used in '58,
is a chore tractor, all-purpose, whatever
you need it for. Hauling manure, feed for cattle.
No hydraulics.

We keep it here in the shed.

the fini-shed
the unaba-shed
the never cra-shed

(though I did roll a little John Deere once)

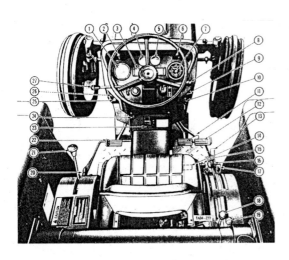

Afternoon the tractors
close the door.
A tractor in a shed is a working thought.

Tractors never far from light
restore themselves rear-end out like
horses facing empty, buzzing
their own dark vapours.

The W-4 Super, identical tractor a year newer. Won't start.

Two-cylinder Blues

You left me in the puni-shed,
the arrowheads of my wheels shot to me,
sorrowheads. And what now but face
the north wall and nothing beyond that.

Some day you gotta come
find me some day you gotta get
beyond this breaking down.

The world's in a corner,
back door open and nothing but
light from me to you.

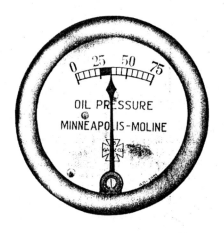

As Long As You Have That Pocket Knife

Lance a boil on a calf
wipe the blade on your pants
peel an apple
wipe the blade on your pants
get the Model R started and
back it out of the shed.

Bought the Model R in '67, centennial year.
Used it in the pig barn for 20 years
hauling manure, hauling feed.

You know you can hear when you hear
tractor through the trees.
The voice of the tractor is the voice of pain
it takes to live in this world.

You know you can see when you see
a dozen versions of the same field,
same stone, same wheel.

You know you can love when you love
to hop onto a tractor, sit there.

You know you can taste when grass tastes
of tomorrow's rain.

You know you can smell when lilacs
remind you of tractors.

Tractors are
attractions this way.

The 140 I bought in 1971.
The hired man, August Tonnies, was the first to use it.
He took good care of it.

Everything original on it.

Front wheels lined up in front of the rear,
it's a row crop tractor
for potatoes and corn in the garden.
The last couple of weeks it's been going every day.

Ever since I realized everything is tractors
the centre of my life turned bountiful,
oilcans in the corners and lost gloves
and a Black Cat tin full of nails.

Tuesday I realized
tractors face any direction and take any.
I phoned all my relatives
and told them I could know
what ails them.

1:56 in the afternoon I realized
last night was just a moment
in one great need. The sky
looks out.

No afternoon can harm me after this.

A mechanic from Outlook is doing the work on the Ford.

I bought it used in Rosetown in 1999.
I just happened to be there.
It's a small, maneuverable tractor
to have on the grounds.
Dedicated front-end loader.

Information Concerning the Removal of the Camshaft

Suppose you want to know the procedure for R&R (remove and reinstall) of the engine camshaft. Your first step is to look in the index under the main heading of ENGINE until you find the entry "Camshaft." Now read to the right where under the column covering the tractor you are repairing, you will find a number which indicates the beginning paragraph pertaining to the camshaft.

To locate this wanted paragraph in the manual, turn the pages until the running index appearing on the top outside corner of each page contains the number you are seeking.

In this paragraph you will find the information concerning the removal of the camshaft.

MAINTENANCE

Periodic Inspections

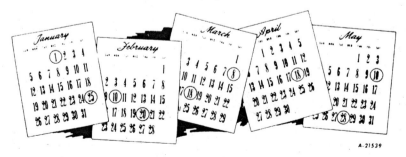

A-21539

Out here at the south edge last year
barley this year summerfallow air
24 in the shade, clouds thrown,
breeze lost in the tall grass. In two weeks condi-
tions change but for tractors only
an hour or two has passed.

This is where the younger tractors
leave the yard for the first time, paint jobs
intact, a full set of tools, high gear,
to teach themselves the field
while the older tractors putter in the yard—
mowing, a hayride, and older yet,
so old even Bernard can't get them going
with his pocketknife, the oldest
tractors of all, having done
their thousand jobs, cloister,
think of themselves as shrines.

I shop around, I don't always get green,
but this John Deere 950 I bought at Humboldt Farm Equipment in 1995.
Run the mowers around the grounds and garden,
sometimes used for spraying.

The roll bar's in case you tip while cutting grass in the ditches.

Trouble Shooting (Again)

Hand throttle not pushed forward:
push throttle forward.

No fuel:
check fuel.

Shut-off valve closed:
open valve.

Slow starter speed:
see "starter cranks slowly."

Cold weather:
use cold weather starting aids.

Improper fuel:
use proper fuel.

Water, dirt, or air in system:
drain, flush, fill, and bleed.

Clogged: replace.

Needs flushing: flush.

Leaks: check for leaks.

Blown: replace.

Engine out of time:
need a professional help for that one,

or see your John Deere dealer.

The Minneapolis-Moline Model RTU, "Minnie,"
is a rowcropper with a hand clutch,
for orchard work, cultivation around trees
and for the bees.

It's the only tractor around here with a dynamo,
the only tractor with one headlight.
Father Xavier drove it for years, he lost the headlight.

Minnie was his legs.
If Minnie was on the fritz, so was Xavier.
If Xavier wasn't feeling well,
better go out and tune up Minnie.

Regional Headquarters of Minneapolis-Moline

Peoria, Ill.
Columbus, Ohio
Omaha, Nebr.
Hopkins, Minn.
Fargo, N.D.
Stockton, Cal.
Memphis, Tenn.
Kansas City, Kansas
Dallas, Texas

and Rosetown, Sask.

Tractor parts in the junkyard live as
angels of repose, comments on art, weed-lives,
homes of wild cats only half (usually the back
half) of which are ever seen.

Smoke from the burn barrel
might as well be fire, exhaling
the cotton fluff of poplar trees
tractors blame on ash.

The 806 diesel was our big tractor at one time,
about 1965. 12,000 hours and it stills purrs along.

We lease it to the organic farm for $5/hour.
(We've got 80 acres organic here, you know.)

The only way to get a tractor to move
without turning it on is to take a bat
and ball to the diamond and hit a few.
The sound of a line drive drives
tractors crazy. They hump
involuntarily, push the weights
from the doors and swing
to the sound of a ballgame.

Each inning the light subsides like
tractors pulling in like shed doors
closing. The score is 3-1 after
three, Red Sox ahead, thanks to
Rauchman's homer in the second
but the Stallions threaten with Ruthven's
towering blast to deep centre and here
tractors have been known to rally in fields,
gear down upon the enemy dugout to show
what a home team means. Sure enough
the Stallions threat disintegrates
and the Red Sox pull away with five
in the fifth, 13-3, mercy, the game's
over. Loehr's the winning pitcher but
it's tractors that won it.

PS:
The losing team is hauled away like scrap back
to the junkyard of their being
where they're known as the Hydraulics
and never win again.

Yessir, it's not uncommon to hang onto tractors
for sentimental reasons.

Part II
The Body of the Tractor

Fig. 8 — The Operator's Leg Should Be Almost Straight When Depressing The Clutch Pedal

A Few Words at First Light

I can't say enough about light once
the dark's rubbed off. If I watch,
it doesn't get here. If I forget,
it shows up. I don't have to pay for it,
don't have to haul it, don't have to decide
to keep it or not. The light is fast
memory I could climb on and ride —
the late '50s, I think it was —
Floyd's Massey-Ferguson
north and east of town.

It's easy to borrow and pay back, light is.
Doesn't take much handling,
don't have to write much down.
It's quieter but packs just as much get-here as trains.
Light lets me know. I'm awake when
I see it between me and
my latest dream.

The light fires me up, but not right now. Let me
finish my tea. Looks like the same
day as yesterday, cloud in it.

I blame light for colour. For a minute there
the world was just me. I blame light for what I see
I've got to get up and do.

In the City of Tractors

He slips on the step of the 970, shoves his assbone up between his ears.
In other words, nuts for earlobes.

Knowing

1

That's the solenoid. It's acting up. Or the alternator
he'd whack with the handle of a brush. That tractor would start,
he'd just know. Always a mystery to me
how he knows.

2

Dad liked the older stuff, kept it in wonderful condition.
I sat around the shed with him. If I asked
what he was doing, he answered, with diagrams,
lots of worn file cards in his pocket and a pen
you had to swear to return.

3

There was no money for a new tractor. But he was
so ingenious, he could build his own parts.
His dad ran a garage in Coderre.

4

I was the knower, home from University at Christmas.
When Dad gave me a hand up to the tractor,
it was a neat sensation. I felt totally safe,
though my knees sometimes wobbled. We hauled
hay to the cattle on a starry night, perfect blackness.

5

After so many years, you notice things
in a field. Tools you've lost. Tipi rings,
arrowheads you'll never find unless
you knew how to see. You notice
things that are different.

In the City of Tractors

You recognize the sound of a tractor in road gear that whine, the bounce and rattle of an implement.
Then you hear him gearing down, coming into the yard. Dad is home, it's meal time.

What You Think About Out on the Tractor

In the field when you start, when you've been off
a self-propelled implement for a while
you think about what you're doing. Otherwise
doze along, try not to fall asleep.

Everything from A to Z because what else is there.
Round and round in ever-decreasing circles
5 miles an hour if you're seeding
or swathing, maybe 1½ to 5
on the combine, depending on the crop (better the crop, slower you go),
up at six, out in the field by eight, go till ten o'clock.

Third of a million for a new John Deere, that's what you think about.

Turn the radio on, listen to the news.
Turn it off after a while.

Maybe you're one of those types who says
when assignments pile up at university
"It will be nice to get back on the tractor
with my mind just ticking over."

You think about politics, what's for supper,
what's on for Saturday night. Or, *Man,
I need a new combine.*

One year we combined flax in December, got our
picture in the *Western Producer,* you think about that.

Or this: *If I won the lottery
I wouldn't be sitting on this stinking tractor.*

And when you come in at night you want
complete silence.

In the City of Tractors

He doesn't know who bought the land, doesn't want to know. *Somebody from Calgary, an agent set it all up.*
He's got until spring. One more harvest, have an auction, sell the big John Deere.

Getting to Tractors

Stan Still's noggin should be photographed in a range
of noggins. His face when he saw it first
this morning had not been folded
neatly the night before. His hands could not
hold water, his throat had thinned, his torso leaned
oh so forlorn.

         That's how Stan
gets to tractors, which lighten his need.
He's a torture of next words until he
sees one coming.

In the City of Tractors

When Dad was about seventeen, he's coming home from the pub when he spots the neighbour's tractor
parked along the road. The neighbour was a bit of a jerk, I should mention. So Dad hops on the neighbour's
tractor, drives it away – in those days, everyone left the keys in the ignition – and hides it in a wooded area.
Turns out this wooded area lies on his own family's land. Next day when the neighbour comes over
to report the loss of his tractor, Dad ends up confessing. A couple of weeks later, after the neighbour has
pressed charges, Dad's got a criminal record, has it to this day. Makes things difficult
when he wants to drive to Minot.

Tractor Exhibition

Entrance

They are Cockshutt, Allis-
Chalmers and Holt. They can be
two storeys tall or small as

a pickup truck. Children dream of sitting
in one. What are we
talking about? The tractor.

○

As you enter, admire photos of tractors
from the last century, at work
in the field pulling ploughs and harrows,

proud owners standing on or near them.
The most recent fit perfectly
our mental image.

○

The older tractors grew
expensive, hot, unwieldy.
What did farmers think of these first

tractors? Reaction was mixed.
Most farmers continued to farm
with what they knew.

○

In the City of Tractors

Bought a wristwatch at the exhibition. Fancy, with a metal bracelet and date function. One day I'm discing 40 acres with the Massey 44. At 10-12 feet wide, that's a lot of rounds on a 40-acre field. I realized my bloody watch was gone. I parked at the next turn, got off, began walking. Damned if I didn't find the watch. Walked only about sixty feet.

Try on a farmer's coat and hat.
Climb onto an old gas tractor, imagine key
moments in tractor history.

Nearby, sit on a tractor seat and compare
the rugged ride of steel wheels to
cushioned rides on rubber.

Decide for yourself
why this improvement
was so popular with farmers.
o
Now it's time
for your dream to come true.
Take the wheel of a John Deere 8500.

In the City of Tractors

He's running the grain auger with his PTO. He engages the clutch, not noticing the tractor is in gear.
The tractor lurches, pulls over the grain auger, which lands on the tractor, missing his face by four inches,
caving in the fender and steering column.

His wife is standing there, watching all this. When he hauls his sorry ass off the tractor, expecting a dose of
sympathy, she ties into him for being so stupid. By the time she's done, he wishes he was dead from the auger.

Tractor Day

We got excited hearing tractors
start up in town. We'd all run
to the biggest, shiniest ones. They looked
monstrous to us kids. *That one's*
not working, we'd hear. Or some old guy
wouldn't let us get on. Some of them
would conk out on the road (the tractors
not the old guys).

In the parade those tractors
shook so bad we chopped up the road about
three feet down. Grease and exhaust, stink,
missing floorboards, a tour around the whole town
and around again to the museum for pie
and tea, all of us waving like stars.

That was *our* day, Tractor Day.
I wanted my boys to see Tractor Day
years later.
                    Were they impressed?
Not like I was.

In the City of Tractors

I met my husband on a bus trip to Dickinson, across the line. Five guys and myself. Things got out of hand, never mind the details. Anyway, here we are. He does the farming work. I phone him, ask *So, how's it going?* *How many laps have you done?* That's what he calls them, "laps". He should be a writer. I've tried to get him to write, but …

Getting Satisfaction

Nothing wrong with tractors.
Helluva lot better than me pulling the cultivator
or lifting the bale. The 1500 Massey 4-wheel drive
runs buggy-sharp, easy as cars
(though the hired man took the motor out
and fucked the clutch up—you couldn't tell him nothing).

Satisfaction is the look of a field when it's done.
A good job done, straight rows. Nothing wrong
with driving tractor but the best thing
is the paycheque I get for sitting on it.

Fig. 30 — Pick A Reference Point At The Other End Of The Field To Help You Drive In A Straight Line

In the City of Tractors

I grew up with them, but was never a horseman. When Dad bought back the farm in 1930, he had power equipment, a brand new IH 2236. A lot of people were shifting over in the '30s from horses. Dad said, "If I had to feed horses in the '30s I'd go broke."

Chapter Quiz I

Angela Lansbury, in her fourth or fifth movie, plays
a widow driving what kind of tractor?

What can you do to both a mountain and a tractor?[1]

Sis scheduled her turn on the big tractor so she could listen to
contemporary hits on AM 1330 Rosetown instead of
crappy 80s music that was usually on. She'd come back
with all the cool songs in her head. How do you think
I felt?

What does a tractor do that a word does?[2]

True or False? Cleanliness is important
to gasoline tractors but is even more important
to diesels.

Who gets the better tractor,
the farmer's son or the hired man?

When we bugged him about skin cancer, Dad tried:
o huge yellow umbrella wedged into the took kit
o woman's straw garden hat
o old ball cap with fabric down the back

---

1 Climb on, at least
2 Makes itself a line

In the City of Tractors

We used our two Case 600s to try to pull the axle off a truck. All we did was break the mounting bolts on the
cab of my 600. The cab slid back, almost took my head off but the steering wheel stopped it.
The truck's axle never did come off.

Tractor Kid Number Seven

I was not that interested in tractors
the summer I turned 16. We had a big garden,
horses, cattle, pigs, and an antique tractor
(no money for a new one) to bale, mow,
till the garden, haul feed. Dad loved it like wind
a row of trees.

        I wasn't that interested
but after a summer on a stoneboat—
rough, unsteady ride, my brother pulling me
on the tractor, the stoneboat made of iron
and heavy timber, no wheels, no runners—
after a summer of that, me hopping off
to pick up a bale, load it on the boat,
hop on, ride to the next bale, later load the bales
into the barn Dad built—I wished I'd taken
an interest in driving tractor, let my brother
bounce on and off that boat.

        But I'm not much interested now.
My dad drove Alice—his Allis-Chalmers, as in
I'm heading out to crank Alice—home to his cottage
at Buffalo Pound, where those who love tractors
notice Dad's inventions, this and that
welded to the frame until Alice
resembles her original form only as curtains
resemble a view.

        I was never that interested,
being the bookish type.

In the City of Tractors

My uncle goes to kill a steer for butchering but has left his .22 at the house. He takes the long yellow wrench off the tractor and smacks the steer between the eyes. Drops him like a rock.

How I Cleaned the Tractor Cab

Nothing else to do on the farm
but putz around, build forts, or fill up
pages in my scribblers with words
and doodles or write in the dirt with a stick.

One bright afternoon in the Quonset,
I noticed a sparrow trapped in the tractor cab.
I closed the door of the cab and called Sylvester
(black, white tips, like the real Sylvester)
who was never far away, he was so tame.
Here's your big chance, Syl, I told him.

The bird was already flapping when I threw
Sylvester in and stood back to watch. The next seven
or eight minutes were messy, all those
feathers and crap. When I opened the door,
Sylvester jumped out, offered me
the dead sparrow and a look that said
What's next, missy? and walked
away. I knew I'd get in trouble,
so I cleaned the cab out good.

SHUT OUT *Wind, Cold, Snow, and Rain . .*

In the City of Tractors

I was cultivating with the 1805 Massey. A high-pressure line to a hydraulic tank broke while I was out there, dumping 30 gallons of oil on the engine, throwing flames and white smoke 20 feet from the tractor. I jumped out, threw dirt on the engine, killed the fire, which I never want to have to do again.

Family Day at the Case-New Holland Dealership

She wasn't sure what part of the body
she climbed on, what model it was, what it meant
under someone's hands. She was proud of the welding
her son had done, but wanted to be alone
with what she thought were thoughts
of her sister's farm near Makwa and their brother
who'd had surgery but was doing well. Her rolled-up
jeans rode up one calf as she leaned onto the tractor
reading a sign.

HOSE INSTALLATION

RIGHT	WRONG

In the City of Tractors
He wanted to get to the dance so bad he hitched up the team to get there, stayed out till sun-up.
When his Dad went out to work he noticed the horses all lathered up and had a few questions for the boy.

(Dream of) My Bride's Demeanour

She hopped from our marriage bed,
pulled me outside a promising day. I thought
I'd made all my promises. The dew had cleared
as an east wind blew us west along
a vehicle track. A *sleepless night,* I said.
Must have been the vitamin C. Or just
the moment, she said, *thousands of them* and
she swerved right as she often did on trails,
by two buildings to a third, a wooden
vehicle shed years ago she'd painted
light blue. I slowed a bit. *Come on,* she said,
pulling open the door and losing
herself inside. What kind of morning
is this, I thought, my bride vanishing,
the day barely awake.

Half of the shed was empty but for broken
glass, scrap. I could already smell
oil on my hands which, I feared, I'd hold
over my face when this was over. Sure enough
I saw in the other half of the shed the glory-deep
red of the 300 Utility, saw the wind outside and tall grass
bending through the door and my bride
driving, her mind on the wheel. I squatted
in the oily dust. *New exhaust pipe,*
I noted, *same old rags.*

Minutes passed, not unpeacefully.
My shoulders loosened, I might have
sighed, now she opened/
closed the toolbox, studied
where everything was. And then she turned
her dark eyes to me.

In the City of Tractors

Got run over by his Versatile 276, broke both his hips and then some. The wheel was turned, the tractor kept
circling. He had to drag himself clear of its path.

Eighteen Miles Southeast of Avonlea

By the time he died in '52, the last pair of Grandfather's horses,
Clydesdales, Mae and Bell, were still around in the pasture,
so soulful you could bring them up next to the rail, leap on,
saunter around the yard, pretending you were outlaws or
other heroes, though as Grandfather reminded us, Mae and Bell
and the rest of the team, now long gone, were the real heroes
of homesteads and proving up *and
keeping us alive those early years. It took
a quarter of the farm to grow their feed but
you talk about backbone, you talk about heart
and horsepower, that's where it comes from,
right there,* pointing at Mae. *Many times
the 18 miles, many times the field.*

He loved those horses so much he didn't
switch over until he first laid eyes on
the 44 Massey diesel, first tractor in the area,
which he soon made his own.

He thought he had the world by the tail.

Now it sits in the machine shed as a novelty item.

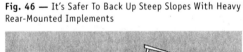

Fig. 46 — It's Safer To Back Up Steep Slopes With Heavy
Rear-Mounted Implements

BACK UP
STEEP SLOPES

In the City of Tractors

As a young man he played ball all afternoon, played accordion in the dance band all night. When he got home,
Dad was just hitching up the horses to head out to the field. The guy was so tired he lay down behind the plough
just after lunch, woke up to see the sun going down.

A Leaf fan, of course. Who wouldn't be?
Forty years since they won the cup is nothing.
I've been farming forty-one.

                     Keon,
Stemkowski and Pappin, Dick Duff,
hard earth Brewer and Baun, how long
can they do the job Stanley, Horton,
Pronovost, Bower, Bruce Gamble, the rest.
I think of them when I summerfallow,
steer curves and slopes, drive the 720
into Hull, knock Beliveau off the puck.

If I had a cab I'd listen to the Leafs
right now if the radio worked.

One of these years, you'll see.

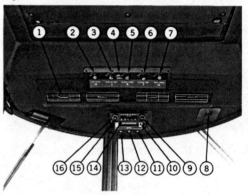

Fig. 34 — Controls In A Tractor Enclosure

1. Air Louver
2. Left Windshield Wiper Switch
3. Air Conditioning Temperature Control Knob
4. Plugged Condenser Indicator Light
5. Blower Switch Knob
6. Heater Temperature Control Knob
7. Right Windshield Wiper Switch
8. Console Lamp
9. Radio Station Selector
10. Tape-Player Channel-Selector Button
11. Tape-Player Tone Control
12. Tape-Player Stereo-Balance Control
13. Tape-Player Volume Control
14. Radio-Tuning Push Button
15. Radio Off-On And Volume Control Knob
16. Radio Tone Control Ring

In the City of Tractors

Age nine or ten, I first drove tractor. I wasn't allowed to pull anything. Dad would give orders about what gear, what rpm. To this day, he still tells me, *Watch those gauges.*

Notes for a Verse Heard on CHAB

Close your eyes and I'll kiss you.
> A farmer's life, if I ever
> heard one, the tractor doing
> the kissing.

Tomorrow I'll miss you.
> Though I haven't checked
> the weather yet.

Remember, I'll always be true.
> Nothing wrong with a man's memory
> when he comes over a rise
> for the fourth or fifth time
> this year alone, a friend
> you don't have to walk to
> to know.

And then while I'm away
> Lake Okanagan so blue
> your wheels ache.

I'll write home every day
> Canada Post? I've seen
> rain that's more on time.

And send
> (wrapped in your favourite colours)

all my loving
> (get that old calligrapher friend of Dad's)

to you
> (to write your name on a cream-coloured card.)

> And that's about it.

In the City of Tractors
Got run over, broke his hips and back and lived, or had a heart attack, fell off dead but
the tractor dragged him around.

Favourite Time of Day

Dad: Quitting time

Daughter: Me too.

Fig. 44 — Power Takeoff For Modern Tractor

In the City of Tractors

Uncle drove a two-ton Ford truck with a grain box, small motor. *Couldn't pull the hat off your head,* was the standard line. For fun, we buried a railway tie behind the truck, attached it to the axle with chains. When uncle was ready to head home, his truck wouldn't budge. We were waiting in the tavern when he showed up moaning that his axle was busted. Most fun of all, we made him buy beer until his story got all the way told.

Chapter Quiz II

Are enclosures designed to buckle, or yield somewhat if the tractor tips over? Why?

When a man on a tractor remembers her, what colours his exhaust?

John Deere & Co. offered a full range of horse-drawn equipment as late as _____.

When a farmer traded in six or eight old geldings, all aged seven with sound teeth,
and drove home a new Cockshutt that made him King Tractor,
what became of the geldings?

How is light like a tractor?[1]

If you're summerfallowing near the slough, dozing along, trying to follow a real good recipe for lemon meringue pie on the radio, what happens?

The hordes of flying ants that bite—who sent them?

---
1 I'm heading toward it right now

In the City of Tractors

Romanian funeral, open casket. The fellow had been driving tractor in road gear, heading home. He comes over a hill on a road that cuts through a slough. For some reason — maybe he falls asleep — the tractor rolls, pins him, and he drowns. 30 years later, four women in a half-ton, all farm women, drive the same road in the dark. Over the same hill. They see a white cow and hit the brakes, leave skid marks on the road. Their truck passes right through that cow at the bottom of that hill. For a long time, they do not travel that road and yes, they are *truly* scared.

Grandma Annie's Holy Book

The big barn, house and chicken barn
at our place formed a U
that piled high with snow. That's where
I learned to drive tractor. It was Dad's
idea. *Go ahead,* he said,
stepping up on the hitch behind me.

Right about then, Grandma Annie
sat down with her bible
in her favourite chair in the living room
as she did every day around noon.
I was driving up the snowhill
in the middle of the yard, Grandma Annie
was reading the Book of Revelation,
getting ready.

Mounting that snowhill, in perfect control,
I was becoming a man on a tractor.
Dad said nothing, didn't need to,
as I paused, put it in gear, and started down.

When things did start to slip,
pushing in the clutch didn't help.
Grandma Annie looked up from her Book
just as I jammed my foot on first the right then
the left wheel brake, sending us into broken
versions of one great spin. Surely the end
was at hand.

Lucky the house was. At the moment
Grandma Annie closed her Book, I crashed
into the southeast corner, not too much damage,
nobody hurt, but Grandma Annie
fell from her chair, she thought dead.

But only miserable, as it turned out.

In the City of Tractors
There's no bad memory that comes from a tractor.

Brags

Sure, well my Massey could pull your
Deere all over the yard.

> You've got a sluggish motor and a rough ride,
> a Monday morning tractor, a bad pod
> of oil, a goddamn piece of fucking junk.

I've got more controls than
the astronauts.

> You're stuck with a lemon, my friend.

I'd rather have winter than
your tractor.

> Two tractors, back-to-back,
> 15 – 20′ of cable or logging chain
> joining them. The loser (that's you) spins
> his tires forward as you're being hauled backward,
> a good crowd of folks to keep score
> and tell about it later.

Every tractor has a role. The Massey
represents everything that's true and good
in the whole dominion.

In the mountains I'd be driving
a train, you'd be
left at the station.

> I might as well plug the auto-steer
> into a horse's ass than bother with
> your Deere.

Anyway, we all
lie like hell.

In the City of Tractors

One old neighbour wore a straw hat during threshing to keep the sun and dust and grain off.
In the end he'd throw the hat in, thresh *it*.

I know farmers so cheap they empty their shoes into the grain truck.

A Hot Issue, 1965

Cab or no cab?

No cab. Cabs are hot, not as much room, not manly. What are you, a chicken farmer?

> Cab. 95 above, pull-type combine, strong tail wind down
> a mile-long field, barley chaff blowing down your neck,
> ears burning, mosquitoes or horseflies like you wouldn't believe —
> all in the past now.

No cab. Can't see good enough from a cab.

> Cab. You're exposed to absolutely everything without one. If you're going
> 4–5 mph and the wind at your tail is going 10, you'd better
> change directions — of the wind if you can. But that won't
> help you with the sun.

No cab. Of three kids, two are going to whine when they can't squeeze in.

> Cab. When we got our first one, oh what a treat.
> Marge would bring me out a cold drink,
> but it was cooler inside the cab.

> The worst thing?
> Air-conditioning gives out.

In the City of Tractors
Mom still laughs about seeing her three little kids pressed up against the glass of the cab.

Windswept

lightrolled
mosquitoscented
pathdrawn
fenceminded
barbbarbed
sadwinded
cattletorn
lusheyed
kneedrenched
mindmended
dreamcrowed
moonlooker
lookhooked
roadholler
pisswatched
nutcoded
ashfooted
woodarmed
underhaired
collarbent
clutchheaded
tractorkidded

In the City of Tractors

I was really young. Dad was out picking up bales by himself, jumping on and off the tractor as it moved.
One time he missed, had to walk home. He got there in so much pain, he lay on the kitchen floor, writhing.
It would take a lot for Dad to do that.

Hope, Part Two

The goddamned Riders should fire the coach
and the GM, get rid of Keith, give Crandall a chance,
get rid of the old guys up front, sack the offensive co-ordinator,
show some imagination, bring in a guy who can play safety,
get themselves a kicker, learn how to play for sixty minutes,
schedule earlier start times, lose the new corporate name
on the stadium, bring back the old uniforms, cut down
on the radio noise between plays, build in
extra parking, let me sip my rum from a thermos
disguised as binoculars, give us a marching band
at halftime, let us run onto the field after the game,
why don't they straighten out the wind
while they're at it, lose the bugs, give us
weather we can count on.

                    I'd drive
in from Humboldt again for that.

Fig. 21 — Don't Drive Half-On, Half-Off The Roadway

In the City of Tractors

When I started school in '59, the old Massey was still around. No power steering. A rock or badger hole would jolt the steering so bad you could break your thumbs.

My great-uncle went blind on a tractor. It was hot, he stopped for a second, looked up. Birdshit landed in his eye.

Difficult Moment with Daughter and Dad in a Field Five Miles SW of Kenaston

What the hell's the matter with you?

      It's on a slant.

Here, let a man do it that knows how.

      There's a hill!

There's no hill.

      There is too!

Fig. 2 — Keep A Constant Watch On The Implement

In the City of Tractors

Dad got arthritis in his neck from looking around at the implements. And arthritis in his driving arm.

My friend the otolaryngologist says he can always tell a farmer because the left ear, closer to the exhaust, will be deafer than the right from turning to look back.

Best Days

60

The first and last ones.

The rest are boring
but boring is good.

That means everything is working.

Fig. 47 — Steer Slightly Uphill To Keep Tractor On Desired Path

In the City of Tractors

A friend is out in his field on his 4890 Case two miles from home, no one else to drive the truck. He puts the Case in low gear and aims it for the yard, then gets in the truck and follows. Half a mile later the tractor engine warms up and picks up speed considerably. He leaps from the truck, starts chasing the tractor, but he's a short little fucker and can barely catch up. He does, though. Jumps on the hitch, maneuvers into the cab, and stops the tractor. All ends well.

Dream of the Smaller Tractor

for Lloyd

I could have told him *I hate this shit* but what was the alternative?

When I was 14 or 15, Dad and I took the big Massey pulling
a hayrack down to the river flat for bales. We loaded
the rack and headed up the hill. Just before we got to the yard
Dad drove over a stone or something, enough to tilt the hayrack
and spill the bales. It began to rain. We built a wall of bales
to sit behind until the rain let up.

I felt uneasy, that close and silent, he was always silent.
You'd think he'd say *Well, since we're stuck here for a while
I'll tell you a story,* but no. No stories, no talk at all.

I used to try to coax a story out of him: *So Dad, you knew
your father better than your brothers did, right?*
Answer: *Nobody knew my father.* No story there.

When the rain stopped we loaded up the bales and carried on.
It was relief to be back sitting on top of the rack.

I was the chore boy—cleaning out the chicken barn,
grinding feed, fencing. Dad was the farmer and I was not.

For years I dreamed of the smaller tractor
and the seagulls and dust, hundreds of seagulls shrieking,
the endless shrieking.

I'd like to haul him out of his grave, make him tell me who he is.

In the City of Tractors

An alcoholic neighbour wanted booze. Someone took his truck keys, so he drove the tractor 15 miles to town.
He came home drunk that night, ran the tractor off the road, broke all his beer. Funny he didn't roll it.
It was an 88 Oliver. No cab.

Cool Water

Too loud to talk, too loud to sing
on the tractor but he hummed
"Tumbling Tumbleweeds" or anything
the Sons of the Pioneers ever recorded,
Irish lullabies, some Tennessee Ernie Ford
and Kenneth McKellar, Sousa marches
in the afternoon when the field grew
longer, just him and the motor and the body
and the rest of the world. He hummed
when he danced, too. This is his
kind of sky, clouds
like slim long arms, air sweet
after rain, cool and
clear
water.

Fig. 33 — Gradually Work Into Wet Spot When Possible

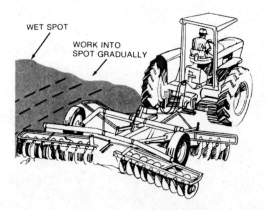

In the City of Tractors

Mrs. N. wants to dig up her daughter Patty and bury her in the family plot in Winnipeg. She calls Grandpa, who agrees to winch Patty out with the Case. The coffin has rotted, but Patty looks pretty good, Grandpa thinks, with her red hair grown long and all. He hitches the chain around her armpits, hoists her out of the grave, then pours himself a shot of courage and sits back to wait for the preacher, and the undertaker with the new coffin.

Stan's Brush with Tractor Greatness

He and pals crossed empty lots
to do homework in each other's
rumpus room, 1960s,
the pingpong table, History, French
and English, study, talk
all the way to grade twelve and the first
year or two beyond when they all take off,
including Stan who returns
a few years later to finish
a diploma and two degrees.

He wants to get out of the city,
get some distance.
He looks in the paper for jobs,
ends up teaching in the city,
takes an apartment next to a bar
full of hollers on game day.

He thought it might be fun. It wasn't.
The place reeked of cheers, bummed-out fans.
He moves to a street where the trees
leak sap on his '82 Corolla
he bought so every Friday
he could drive to the lake or every workday
to school, brand new elementary, grade seven,
in his class a girl, Sue,
dropped off by her mother, Edna,
whose own mother, Edna Sue,
is a Massey.

Fig. 13 — Drawbar In Extended Position

Fig. 14 — Drawbar In Retracted Position

In the City of Tractors

Because no one could babysit, I'd be crammed in behind the seat in the cab. Getting my head bounced around hurt after a while, so I put an icecream bucket on. Not so much for protection but to make a statement: *I'm here, do I need a pail on my head to remind you?*

Chapter Quiz III

Do you ever wish you weren't alone
so much on the tractor?

Is "I Still Feel
Vibrations" about
getting off?

Approaching a crossroad which way
will Basil on the 950 turn?

Is it where you're
coming from or
going to?

If mom was sick, so Dad had to pull the baby in a wagon behind the seed drill,
leaving him at the end of the field, asleep in the wagon,
how long would it take Dad to get back to check?

Does the machine
= the man?

What kind of sandwiches did I
take out to dad?

Fig. 35 — Dig Behind The Wheels To Allow Backing Out Of Mire

In the City of Tractors

Uncle Bill used the new chainsaw he was so proud of to take out a caragana hedge. He dug, cut around the
roots with the saw, set it down, hitched a chain around the roots, and pulled the whole hedge out with the
tractor but ran over the chainsaw.

Why Stan Still Never Makes It Past Swift Current

Which way are the mountains? is a line
Stan read in *Dennis the Menace* years ago. A better
question, *why?* Driving past the ripening
to Moose Jaw is enough, fields that lead
to a Case dealership on the east side so smoothly
he forgets who he is but not when. 5:30
barely a car wakens the road. His passengers sleep,
less so since Stan tuned in
Santana on CHAB.

Stan won't complain about mountains but won't
sing about them either. Clouds that terrify,
air so pure you grin, light that turns a corner,
repeats itself, the Bow its own view. Lucky
for valleys or mountains wouldn't breathe.

Anyway Stan isn't there yet. He's here
where days come from, sunny and warm.
No risk, the weather, but clouds ahead
leak and blur, draw the deepest
colours from the land, dugouts keeping
an eye on things—Ernfold, Morse,
a tractor for sale near Herbert.

Anything more to add,
Stan will let you know.

In the City of Tractors

All we talked about at dinner was the tractor. It was always breaking down. Should be bring a mechanic out?
Should be fix it ourselves? Usually we fixed it ourselves. If you had to calla mechanic for everything,
it would bankrupt you.

That's what you do in winter when there's nothing else to do – fix something.

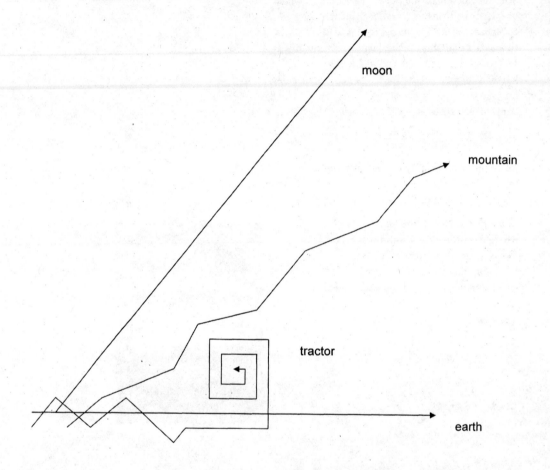

In the City of Tractors

I was 15. July, hot, a day like today. When we finished summerfallowing, we shut down for supper and went home. At supper we heard this roar in the distance, like a waterfall three or four miles north of the house. It was the Great White Swather, a foot of hail, pounding down hard enough to kill livestock, pulverize everything. Nothing was left but a wall of steam by the time we drove up there. We'd been planning a fishing trip to Madge Lake to see who could fish and who couldn't. But the hail wiped out harvest, wiped out the fishing trip.

Stan Still's Mountain Ideas

He tries to remain steady
but he's beaten by the views.

o

The Banff Springs — now *that*
he can relate to, taking his bride there
if he had a bride. Stan checks in.

o

For two days he hardly leaves his room,
finally takes his shoes off, settles back
in a white chair on the open sixth-floor lounge
and gives himself ten words to
hop into this view
        breathe and
                that's ten.

o

He can't sleep because
he feels as if he's lying
on the side of a mountain too exposed
or too hidden. He can't put his head
all the way down.

A decent blue today left
tread-shaped slashes
at the edge of what he sees.

o

Walking along the highway
only a half mile from the hotel,
one eye on that deer's
one eye on him, Stan turns into
the trees.

In the City of Tractors

It was just time, his dad says, now that he's sold the land where he's livedhis whole life. *I still love the work
but we can't make money anymore.*

o

Though Stan is afraid of heights
he's not afraid of mountains
and enjoys standing still on a path
until he's moved
one way or the others.

o

He strides a path
same way he boots along a furrow
for the edge of his field
careful not to get lost
unless *twisted wide open*
was the same as *lost.*

o

As long as he can holler
and keep what he knows behind him
he's ok.

The treemass falls, rises.
In a couple of steps he's ready
to round that corner
where he can't be seen but where
he has to be to see Bow Falls.
He feels rushed, turns back,
heads down the highway's
narrow edge to a blind corner,
safe at last.

o

As for bears,
he'd rather meet a tractor.

o

In the City of Tractors

I was about 17. I came home after being out all night, just in time to start work. I started up the tractor and fell asleep. It ran for two hours before Dad found me sleeping and I found myself in deep shit.

Animals See Tractors All the Time

Just this morning I came across her.
Her mother had hidden her in the weeds.
Young, could barely walk.
I stopped to let her get away.

deer moose antelope

I was just about finished,
working around some bush,
when I picked up a deer horn: flat tire.

fox den

East of the house but
we weren't allowed near it.

geese rabbits

Baby rabbits, size of your palm. My brother
caught Spike in the field, gave him a home
on campus in Saskatoon.

skunks

Ran one through
the combine a few times.
The trick is not to stop.
Keep the straw going.
It flushes out the smell pretty good.

porcupines badger our dog Skippy

He followed the tractor round and
round and round, later collapsed
in the barn, just played right out.
Slept for twelve hours.

birds

In spring you often see nests
in the stubble, see the nest,
carefully go around it.

pairs of coyotes
mice and voles
hawks

Always fun to watch them
hanging around behind the tractor.

The rest is just horsefly.

In the City of Tractors

I rode a lot of old, ugly tractors as a kid. Dad had a two-cylinder JD. Just pounded it all day, low rpm, reliable as hell.
He said, "I like the open tractor because I can listen to the birds," which is a lie because you can't hear a thing.

Humpback Whale Dream

His body is not sure of the light. Oh yes, a mountain
empties his way, in his direction.

On the tractor he is able to leap from the field,
fully free of it. The engine is a masked unit
a careful observer can distinguish from others
by the unique pattern of its lived and varied edges.
The moment the tractor lifts from the field is one
ton of wonder, dust a splash. Just once, this happens.

He lies in bed until the best of it fades. 6:40,
time to get going.

In the City of Tractors

Taking a shortcut, I drive the Versatile 900 into a slough. It sinks out of sight. I have to get another tractor
with a rock picker to haul in enough rock for traction. Takes me six hours to get the bastard out of there.

Some of these wet springs, it's normal to get stuck. Everybody gets stuck, trying to get that last foot in.

Stan's Tractor Story

A friend urged me to jot
a few things down out here
when you have a moment to
spare ha ha and at first
I thought well ok can't
hurt too much in a spiral-bound
notebook the size of my hand.

Next I've put some Duke Robillard on
the cd player in the cab and I'm
kicking back in the northeast corner,
writing a few words, about forty
or so, remembering one time,
north edge of a barley field
parallel to the tracks when a train
came up beside me. I never heard him
till he gave me a blast, scared the shit
right out of me.

Turned out to be another
way of knowing, the notebook,
and the book my friend gave me,
Charles Simic *The Voice at 3:00 A.M.*
which I read, two or three pages at a time.

In the City of Tractors

Uncle had a hired man, a kid I'd gone to school with. He's hauling a cultivator with Uncle's Deere. I follow
in the half-ton. He stands up in the cab, opens the back window to flick his cigarette butt toward me and
starts showboating. Pretty soon the tractor is veering toward the ditch. I'm pointing like crazy.
He finally catches on, just in time.

He was so scared he gave up smoking.

Chapter Quiz IV

*Are the sounds and activities the participants sense
really happening, or are they a fictional construct?*

When is four wheel drive untrue?

Is it dog-eared or
do-geared? *Plow* or
plough?

What are the three standard power takeoff arrangements?

You want to get out of farming but can't bear to tell your Dad,
who doesn't want anything else. What do you do?

When you go to the mountains you
won't get caught in a cloud, eh?

What happens to the gearshift of a Massey 40 after
45 years?

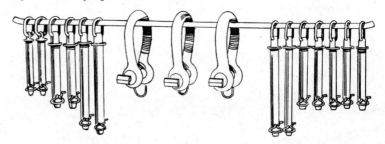

Fig. 5 — Use Only High Grade Hitch Pins

In the City of Tractors

When you're a kid, you're your father's son. Now I help in peak periods. In 25 years since I've lived in the city
we've become friends, Dad and I. In the morning, we drive out to service the implement where we left it in
the field overnight. That initial start-up, diesel smell, piston-slap — all part of the conversation.
We chew the fat, plan the day ahead.

Four Ways, Leaving the City of Tractors

In the city of tractors
I'm older on a rowboat.
Tractor still, boat in motion,
sun fires down, hauls
cloud. A motor
cuts out over walleye.
In stillness we're all running down.

°

In the city of tractors
you'd rather she didn't leave
for the city today. You just started
to know the small body
turned up in your mind.

°

In the city of tractors
your arms and back do the work.
You lower your cap, watch where you've been.
You bring it in near sunset.

°

In the city of tractors
half a bottle of red wine
on some dresser, some buffet
in last and first of a day's light.

Part III
July, Two Years Later

Monk, Farm Manager Dies

MUENSTER, Sask. —

Brother Bernard Henry Lange, OSB, long-time manager of St. Peter's Abbey farm, died May 30 of an apparent heart attack while on a fishing trip in the Meadow Lake area.

The son of Bernard Lange and Anna Nienaber, Lange was born in 1929, at Watson, Sask., and took his primary schooling at Harvest School between St. Gregor and Annaheim. At 18 he joined the monastic community at Muenster and made his first profession of vows before Abbot Severin Gertken, OSB, on March 21, 1949, and final profession on March 21, 1952.

Lange spent two years as janitor in St. Peter's College before beginning work on the farm. In 1965 he began a two-year course in agriculture at the University of Saskatchewan. As manager of the farm since 1971, Lange was well-known to the hundreds of people who came in the fall for vegetables and fruit. His expertise in handling machinery, in the repair shop, in water management, heating and plumbing will be greatly missed.

His partners at the card table in the abbey recreation room will greatly regret his absence. His fellow monks are especially grateful for his faithful presence during the daily hours of prayer in chapel.

—adapted from *Prairie Messenger,* June 16, 2004

Gerry Hill:

76

Two summers ago in the heat
Bernard took us around one afternoon,
backed each tractor into the sun for Shelley
to photograph, Bernard telling me
about the tractors, when he bought them,
from whom and for how much,
what they've been used for all these years.
Some he had to crank to start. One tractor
was out in the field and he showed us
that one the next day. He must have wondered
what we were doing but he obliged so freely.
That's him on the 806.

A Wind that Changes Sunday

East wind or something, I forget, remembers
the clouds, hordes a few as cumulus. Trees
air out, a verbing wind, phenomena
raw as possible as if nothing
makes any sense.

Junkyard, the longest memory, stacks
its eyes and watches, sure that this
moment's eternally new, a day
of multiple forces at rest, visiting day
cars come and go.

Day of water land air and creatures
that pick any two, welcome to
my neighbourhood the grebes, day of ruts,
dried tractor tire *K*s and broken *Y*s.

And under thunder a train,
a carcass of rain, the dark
a.k.a. bottom side of clouds,
rain getting down to it.

Abbot Peter:

I met Bernard in '58 when I came to St. Peter's to school.
I relied on him for the farm and all it involved over there.
In addition to his usual jobs, he'd fill in on Sundays
with the dairy herd, milk morning and evening, plus the hogs, chickens.
He was a hard worker with a good pool of practical knowledge,
but he knew his limitations. If he couldn't fix it, he'd get someone
who could.

Bernard was a patient man, ready to interrupt
his own schedule to help you. And he was wily, knew how
to negotiate a deal. I always thought we had
way too many tractors and did we need
another one?

He loved Skat, the card game we played
in the community after evening meal.
He'd played it for 40-50 years at least.
He always kept track in his head, I couldn't figure out how.

With his heart problems, Bernard needed to slow down.
He'd been in hospital a month around Christmas.
There was an incident just after that. A power line broke,
started a grass fire. Bernard went out. I went
to help him, didn't think he should be working alone.
I found Bernard with a shovel putting it out. It wasn't a big fire,
but he was panting.

He finished spring work on Wednesday, took off fishing on Thursday
as he did every spring, with three-four others near Meadow Lake.
They fished on Friday. Saturday afternoon some high school
kids were out, everyone was having a good time. That night he died.
He'd been feeling good that week.

I checked his alarm clock after he died. It was set for 4:30.

Roger Berting:

It was Bernard who welded
an extra step on the 806 so
Peter, age 80, could climb up.
I helped design it but
Bernard did all the work.

Peter:

It looks factory-built?
Did you see it?

Demetrius:

He changed the oil on the all the vehicles,
serviced the heavy equipment,
could make anything run.

That blue truck is his.

Fire Wrecks Shed at St. Pete's

by Keri Dalman, *Humboldt Journal* Editor, June 10, 2004

A small fire in a vehicle escalated into a four-alarm fire at St. Peter's Farm by Muenster last week, destroying a machine shed and its entire contents.

It was very early—about 12:40 a.m.—on June 2 when the Humboldt and Muenster fire departments were notified of the blaze on the farm, which is located on the same grounds as St. Peter's College and Abbey.

However, when fire crews arrived on scene a few short minutes later, there wasn't much left to save of the 3,000 square-foot shed.

"By the time we got there, it was fully involved," said Humboldt Fire Chief Norbert LeBlanc, adding that the roof of the building had already folded in.

The fire completely destroyed everything, he indicated. "Nothing was salvageable." The total cost of the damage LeBlanc estimated at $200,000.

Lost in the fire were two tractors, two three-ton trucks, a square baler and a mix mill. A Morris air seeder, parked next to the building, also suffered some heat damage. Luckily, no other buildings were damaged, nor people injured in the fire.

LeBlanc believes the fire originated in one of the three-ton trucks. They're not sure yet exactly why the truck started on fire, he said, but it did, and eventually the flames spread to the rest of the building.

The heat of the fire was extremely intense, he added, because the building was encased in steel.

"It was like an oven—it contained the heat," he said. "Plus, the front and back doors of the building were open, so the fire had all the oxygen it needed to keep burning."

The two departments—about eight firefighters from Muenster and 15 from Humboldt—spent two hours on the scene, putting water on hot spots.

The fire was reported, LeBlanc added, when people heard the banging of the tires on the vehicles exploding.

Abbot Peter:

Randy, the pressman, had printed the Messenger a day early
so they could go to Bernard's funeral next morning.
He was in to clean the press, cycled home about midnight.

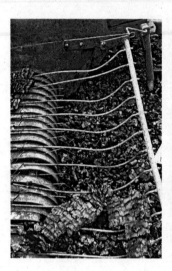 

Randy:

It was a nice evening, one of the few we'd had.
I decided to have a beer and some chips on the deck.
I noticed a crackling, swishing sound,
coming from the farm so I walked down my lane,
could see smoke rising and flames, thought it might be
the trees. I phoned the Abbot and walked down
the lane again. Hearing increased noise and explosions,
I now realized it was the machine shed, called 9-1-1
and walked over to have a look. Muenster Fire Department
came, then Humboldt F.D. They couldn't save anything
from the shed but prevented the fire from spreading.

Mandy (who looks after the chickens on the farm):

Bernard was a brother, more than just a monk.
We always did things together.

We stayed up at my house, my acreage
four miles north of Rapid View near the lake.
We fished on Friday, the men went out Saturday morning.
Saturday afternoon was my grandson's grad
that's why we went there.
That night Bernard was so happy.
I used to tuck him in at night,
sit beside his bed. We'd pray
together or just talk.

In the morning he usually made breakfast,
had coffee going, had been for a walk,
I'd be up when he got home but this morning
he was still in bed. I didn't want to look in
and when I did, I knew he was gone.

I shouldn't say this about a monk but
I loved him. We had what
nobody else in the world had.

Roger Berting:

Different around here without Bernard?
Like night and day. I've got to do
his job and mine—go to the elevator,
pick up parts. Right now we're buying
a new truck, not having much luck.
And we need a new front-end loader tractor.

We had supper in the field on Wednesday, that was when
we finished seeding. Bernard said "Going to pick
some stones?" I said "Done already." He said
"Oh, now we can relax" and he went
fishing on Thursday. I talked to him
Saturday night, got the phone call Sunday.

He was just about the most important person out here.

He leaves a big hole.

I don't know what's going to happen.

Demetrius:

Minnie's fine.
She's hitched to a flatbed over at the fire pit.
The choir kids want their pictures taken.
Oh no, she's fine.

Might need a new battery,
though, [shrug]. She won't
take a charge.

Sometimes I have to crank her.

Ray DeMong:

Bernard died May 30, I think.
The fire was the following Tuesday, I think.
Wood walls on the shed, tin roof
came down on everything.
First thing we had to do was pull it off.
The fire started in one of the trucks,
burned hotter on one side.

Gerry Hill:

Ray had spent 15 hours fixing the baler and swather
in return for the two burnt tractors and other
scrap iron. First Brother Randy stripped the chassis
of whatever he thought hadn't burned. Now Ray's son Girard
is hauling the scrap to his acreage.

> *(Marliss, writer: What kind of tractors?*
> *Brenda, writer: Burnt tractors.)*

They haul the burned truck chassis onto the flatbed,
using a winch to pull and the Ford
tractor with its front-end loader to push,
Ray with a crescent wrench on what's left
of the steering column guides the approach
to heavy ramps at the back of the flatbed.

Girard's uncle, a monk, Father Lawrence, says
Girard is an electrician, one of those farmers
always looking for a better way to do something
and he gives examples which I can't remember right now.
Girard's got a bad back. Couldn't sleep last night
he worked so hard yesterday, cramping up his back
to crawl around through the iron. Look,
you can see it in the way he walks.

List of 14 Tractors Owned, 2004

1 1984 Steiger Cougar CM-250
in the large quonset

2 1996 John Deere 8100
in the field

3 1974 International Harvester 784
burnt

4 1975 John Deere 4430
burnt

5 1955 International Harvester 300 Utility
in a two-shed with the Ford

6 1968 International Harvester 724 Diesel
in a shed with rake

7 1949 McCormick W-4 Standard
in the four-shed down by the old house

8 1950 McCormick W-4 Super
the four-shed

9 Minneapolis-Moline Model R
the four-shed

10 International Harvester Farmall 14
the four-shed

11 Ford 2000
in a two-shed with the 300

12 John Deere 950
in the vehicle shed

13 1946 Minneapolis-Moline Model RTU
down by the bees

14 International-Harvester 806
in the organic shed

Ray DeMong:

The baler gave us some trouble because
the front-end loader tractor, the Ford,
broke down, a busted coupler, so finally
my son and I took the pump assembly
apart. Man, somebody had messed it up
pretty good. We made a new one,
raided another baler for wheels and tires,
pushed it onto the trailer.

Abbot Peter:

The fire happened after the wake but before the funeral.
I had to scramble to prepare the homily
that night, stayed up late but got it done.
I thought about referring to the fire but decided
not to, saw it as extraneous.

Shed Fire: An Inventory

rusted truck cab
    face down, abandoned, both doors
    flung out

dashboard
    vacant, mouths broken open

pedals
    some burning reversal stuck aloft or
    fused solid to the floor

found art
    rust figures char
    won't ever burn

the wire built into tires
    broken in wild coils
    sprayed like grass
    moment unknown

roofing
    overcooked lasagna noodles
    enlarged fifty thousand percent
    turned to metal and burned

gears of the baler
    victim of too much motion

found part
    sp_d_ h_ndl_

whatever else
    cloud-shaped mass of melted
    aluminum sawn-off exhaust
    pipes steering wheel

Abbot Peter:

> *On the Farm Board, three members including me.*
> *We've discussed succession on the farm*
> *and now we have to make some decisions.*
> *Bernard wanted to work as long as he could.*
>
> *We don't have a monk who can take over—*
> *Basil could but he's looking after something else.*
>
> *Do we hire someone? Rent the land?*
> *We have to decide.*
>
> *Roger is a full-time employee. He can take care of it for this year.*

Demetrius:

> *Don't worry, we'd never sell the land.*

Tractor Note

One pass of the cultivator turns
a thirty-foot width of new air.
The east quarter will be done by noon.

The difference between new summerfallow
and old is one of softness and noise
between 8 and 11 o'clock, five or six extra
degrees, what is new and what
like everything hardens.

The 8100 only by grace of oil change
survived the fire which claimed the 784 and
the 4430. It finally makes
a second pass on its way back to the yard,
gulls swallowing its wake.

Later in the day it stands warm
from the tremors of the field.

Shed Fire: A Few Views

1
day after the day the site is empty and burned,
cotton fluff moving in
sky never bluer, a breeze

2
one drive-in theatre always open,
rusted-out concession stands, pillars
speakers severe in their dread,
the screen burned away but for its frame

3
open house
doorways ruined

4
movement given two weeks to live,
coils ready but how much
summer left in their spring,
struts hanging free,
the arm of a wiper blade all the flesh

5
any four of you could pick
a stand of lockers and chat
hanging up your burnt coats

6
the *ka-ticky* bird rules
with the *syoot-syoot* and friends
and the hoodoo poplars flickering

7
tall grass around the concrete
foundation of the shed (all that remains)
awaits word its growth plan goes ahead

8
chain killing event
rusted bolt shrine to the Blessed Virgin event
two-metre exhaust pipe cut-off event
strip the New Holland 359 event

9

and for the woman whose good friend has died
the site is surrounded by work
she did with him—flowers,
grass, the shrine, card games
in the shop without a window
but plenty of light inside, the two of them

10

nothing can
enter here now

11

the remains of the shed absorb
deeper into the mind
every time a monk cycles by

tractor keeps sound
alive endless Basil takes the kids
on the 300 Utility gear down
up backroads out buildings Ken gets
the wagon full of tables for
the barbecue currents
of grass Demetrius
gets on Minnie morning
afternoon comicosmic hum-hustle Ray's
on the Ford boosting scrap iron
onto his trailer Brother Peter
on the Farmall tending corn empty
steering wheel sky tractors
beat deeper than we know in burrows
their motor wriggles through Pete
on the 806 baling like a couple
of trains a tractor back the Steiger
rutting in the east field someone
hauled picnic tables to the
perennial garden one
continuous tractor except Sunday

Abbot Peter:

Let us pray:

Father, have mercy on your servant Bernard, and grant that we will come together in joy in your kingdom of love and peace.

May he and all the faithful departed, through the mercy of God, rest in peace. Amen.

Acknowledgements

Shelley Sopher and her photographs shared my first steps toward *14 Tractors* and provided ongoing inspiration. All photographs were taken by Shelley except those on pages 42, 44, and 70 (Brenda Schmidt), and pages 65, 83, 89, and 91 (Gerry Hill).

Steven Ross Smith, Brit Matthews, and Brenda Schmidt gave earlier parts of this manuscript a good reading.

A tip of the cap to my technical consultants, Mark Duke and Gordon Gardiner.

This book would not exist without the stories people told me so generously. A grateful tip of the cap to Leroy and Dennis Alm, Wallace Cochlan, Mark Duke, Bernice Friesen, Don Gardiner, Gord Gardiner, Elizabeth Greisman, Carla Hancock, Shelley Leedahl, Rhonda Litzenberger, Cliff Lobe, Annette Marche, Brit Matthews, Wynne Nicholson, John Penner, Lloyd Ratzlaff, Brenda Schmidt, Harvey Schmidt, Mitch Spray, and Susan Stinson.

The first question in "Chapter Quiz IV" was found in a description of Janet Cardif's "Forest Walk" at the Walter Philips Gallery, The Banff Centre.

"Tractor Exhibition" consists of text found in the "Current Tractor Exhibitions" section of the Canada Agriculture Museum website (www.agriculture.technomuses.ca).

The Banff Centre and Saskatchewan Writers/Artists Colonies at St. Peter's Abbey and Emma Lake provided three writer-friendly homes away from home.

I'm grateful for the support, institutional and personal, of Luther College at the University of Regina and for a grant from the Humanities Research Institute, University of Regina.

Additional illustrations have been reproduced by permission of Deere & Company, John Deere Publishing, 1974. All rights reserved.

Thanks to Douglas Barbour, Lou Morin, Tiffany Regaudie, and Natalie Olsen at NeWest Press for starting *14 Tractors* with me.

Born in Herbert, SK, Gerald Hill has lived in Papua New Guinea, Calgary, Rocky Mountain House, Saskatoon, and Edmonton. He completed a B.Ed from the University of Calgary, a diploma in Creative Writing at David Thompson University Centre in Nelson, BC, and an MA in English at the University of Alberta. He teaches English and Creative Writing at Luther College at the University of Regina.

Published widely in literary journals and anthologies, Gerald Hill has written four previous poetry collections: *Heartwood, The Man from Saskatchewan, Getting to Know You,* which won the Saskatchewan Poetry Award in 2004, and *My Human Comedy.*

He's never driven a tractor.

The production of the title **14 *Tractors*** on Rolland Enviro 100 Print paper instead of virgin fibres paper reduces your ecological footprint by :

Tree(s) : 2
Solid waste : 139 lb
Water : 1,315 gal
Suspended particles in the water : 0,9 lb
Air emissions : 306 lb
Natural gas : 319 ft^3

Printed on Rolland Enviro 100, containing 100% post-consumer recycled fibers, Eco-Logo certi-fied, Processed without chlorinate, FSC Recycled and manufactured using biogas energy.